DON'T LET

Your Wedding

BE THE DEATH OF YOU

The Shocking Truth About Wedding Planning

DAVID ANTHONY, WEDDING M.D.

© David Anthony

ISBN: 978-1-54396-266-6

WHAT THE BRIDES (AND GROOMS) ARE SAYING

The attention to detail was outstanding and it was very evident that David went above and beyond. Every staff member, from servers to the bartenders, was polite and professional. I would not hesitate to recommend this place to anyone. I was skeptical because of the location, but boy was I wrong.

—Barb

We want to give a HUGE thank you to David for helping us plan the best day of our lives. Everything was absolutely on point! Anything we needed you did, no questions asked! Thank you so incredibly much! We absolutely recommend this venue for your wedding day!!

—Kristen

I didn't have a single complaint the whole night. David was even out there serving food with the staff. I had an amazing night and I thank everyone at Dibble's Inn!

—Jason

I have loved working with Dibble's Inn. David was so helpful with planning and organizing our special day! The venue choices were all great and every option on the menu was delicious. So excited to get married here!

—Greg

My husband and I just got married on Friday and it was the wedding of my dreams! David went above and beyond in every aspect. I truly couldn't have asked for a better experience.

—Renee

Our wedding was perfect and Dave was very accommodating. Jitters and nerves about things going according to script are normal for everyone. But the crew came through in a big way for us and we'll never forget it. We were the first ceremony to be held in the Grotto and the owner made it happen. Thank you to everyone on the entire staff for making it an event that my bride and I will remember forever.

—Dave

Dave and the staff did a wonderful job for my daughter's wedding. Always there to answer questions and to make sure we had everything we needed. Thank you so much for everything. It was truly a beautiful day.

—Margaret

We can't even begin to express both our love and gratitude for all of the Cannery staff! David thank you for making this possible.... I got compliments all night from friends and family saying it was the most beautiful wedding they have ever been to! The food was awesome as well! Everything was perfect; highly recommended!!!

—Nikkita

Working with Dave and Barb was fantastic. They are such fun and kind-hearted people. Dave was there the day of my wedding making sure everything was perfect. When planning a wedding (and being a perfectionist), it's so great to work with other perfectionists. And that is exactly what Dave is. He made me feel so confident in his staff, the venue, and even a little better about the outside temperature (NEGATIVE 26). He even made sure the outside fire pit was lit. It was a beautiful touch that was appreciated by many!

—Jessica

I highly recommend this venue. I really can't say enough about how AMAZING this venue and the staff were for our wedding 8/17/18. First of all, the venue itself is absolutely beautiful and nothing like any venue I've seen around here, which is one of the reasons we fell in love with it in the first place.

—Kiona

Well, it happened!! Thank you so much, David, for making it amazing. My guests couldn't stop raving about how it was such a unique venue and the best wedding they have ever been too. David and Joanne were the most fun people to work with. They let me get away with my crazy ideas and all. If you're looking for a venue that's not your normal wedding venue, check it out! You won't be disappointed! Joanne went above and beyond for me, always trying to make sure I was happy and so was everyone else. Thank you, guys. I love you!!!!!!!! Xoxoxo!

—Jessica

We had our wedding on Saturday and it was beyond perfect! The venue is absolutely stunning. We had exceptional service and the food was delicious! Everyone is still raving how unique and beautiful it was.

They keep stating it was one of the best weddings they have ever been too! We want to give a HUGE thank you to David for helping us plan the best day of our lives. Everything was absolutely on point! Anything we needed, you did, no questions asked! Thank you so incredibly much! We absolutely recommend this venue for your wedding day!!

—Krissy

David never once overlooked even a small detail and took care of everything. Sadly, the night came to an end, but even that part was made so easy with the help of the team at The Cannery. They packed everything up and made sure it was safely loaded into cars. Speaking from very recent experience, planning a wedding gives you plenty of reasons to stress, but the team at The Cannery will put you at ease. They are incredibly professional and on the day of make you feel like yours is the only wedding of the year. I can't even count the number of compliments and texts we've received saying things like, "best wedding ever," "amazing night," and so on. Book your wedding at The Cannery!

—Katelynn

DEDICATION

This book is dedicated to the thousands of brides that have trusted me with their wedding day. I will forever be grateful to all of you for having the faith in me to carry out your vision. I want you all to know how seriously I take it and how hard my staff and I work to make sure your day is perfect. I work just as hard for you as I would for my own daughters. You all have a special place in my heart.

Thank you, Barb, the owner of PWV, and all of her staff; a special thank you to Joanne, Pam, Annalee, Renee, Danielle, Holly, Ralph, and Mary Ann. Thank you all for working with me to make every wedding perfect.

Thank you to Chef DeBarr and Chef Rowe and your incredible staff. You are the best in the business. A special shout out to Sous Chef Rich and Shawna.

Thank you to Justin and Jim for all that you do. Always there to answer the bell. You guys are amazing.

And to our future brides, you will always get all that we have. We strive to make every wedding perfect.

CONTENTS

The more you invest in marriage,
the more valuable it becomes.

—Wedding M.D.

ACKNOWLEDGEMENTS

I have been very blessed in my life to experience very little loss of the people that are most important to me. Other than my grandparents, I haven't lost anyone that has shaped my life. Something that I have wanted to do for a very long time and always put off is to sit and write a letter to thank the people that have shaped my life. So what better time than this. Obviously, my parents have been amazing and did the best that they could to provide. I will forever be grateful for everything you have done.

However, when I think about the success I have experienced in my life, and humbly I say it has been more than one person deserves, I think of a specific group of people. Some of you may not even remember me. Some spent short periods of time in my life and others have been around way too long (haha).

So here is the list:

Chuck Crist	Janet Lansing	Carl Gomore	Carlo Stirpe
Joe Goss	Jim Moretti	Bob Campbell	
Ed Williamson	Buddy Wleklinski	Scott Taroff	
Bill Holthoser	Gary Graham	Joel Adour	

Thank you all so much. You all will never know the profound effect you have all had on my life. The life lessons I have learned from each of you along the way have been invaluable. I have never forgot the lessons you all have taught me. The advice, the lessons, the ass chewing, the council, and just who you are as people have given me great direction in my life. It has always been the reason I push so hard. You all are the reason I have enjoyed success in my life. You are the reason why my daughters don't want for anything. I am so blessed to have had you all in my life. And one last time, THANK YOU, THANK YOU, THANK YOU!

www.premierweddingvenuescny.com
david@pwvcny.com

INTRODUCTION

So Why Write a Book?

What I have found over the years is that brides all go through the same anxieties. It is all based on the unknown. Girls grow up thinking about this day their entire lives. But when it comes time to pull it off, they have no idea how.

In order to take the pressure off and avoid the feared BRIDEZILLA, I wanted to create an easy-to-read guide for planning a wedding, a guide that educates the brides about what to do and what to avoid. The topics will cover everything from picking the venue, choosing vendors, questions that should be asked, and little tips and tricks to just help you through the process. The one thing that I hear all the time is "This is the first time that I've done this." Well rest assured that this is not the first time that I've done this. So let the 3,000-plus weddings that I've worked on lend that experience and help guide you through this journey. So here we go!

*People are weird.
When we find someone
with weirdness that is
compatible with ours, we
team up and call it love.*

—Dr. Seuss

1.

NO MORE NORMAL

I want to start by talking about how weddings have changed and, boy, have they. In the last 10 years, Pinterest has changed the wedding industry and moms especially struggle with the changes. Remember, as I said earlier, every little girl grows up dreaming about their wedding. But the problem is, SO DOES HER MOM. Mom has her own vision for her little baby's wedding. Well, unfortunately, mom isn't keeping up with the trends like her little girl and the process that she had followed has drastically changed.

We now live in a world of visuals, not traditions, and therein lies the problem. Mom and grandma have done the same things at every wedding they have been to for their entire lives. So let's say that mom is 55 years old and grandma is 85 years old. That means for 50 years and 80 years, the two of them have done the same exact wedding over and over and over. Therefore, they want to take that process and push it into today's formula. The problem is that this doesn't really work and it creates a point of contention between the mother,

Love doesn't make the world go round; love is what makes the ride worthwhile.

—Elizabeth Browning

grandmother, and bride, as they try to stick a round peg in what's now become a square hole. The old timeline has changed, so let's talk about what it used to be versus what it is today.

What Has Changed

1. *The Church*

The way it worked for years and years was that you would arrive at the church in the morning, and sometime around noon, you would have the ceremony.

Then in the evening, five or six o'clock, you would go to a reception hall and have the reception. For the five hours in between the ceremony and the reception, the guests would go to a relative's house. They would eat some food and mingle, while waiting for the bride and groom to take pictures and finish remaining tasks. Finally, the reception begins. Well, **that no longer happens**! Most of the time couples are getting married at a venue. When they do decide on a church, it's mainly because of outside pressure. Now I am not saying one is wrong or right, but the timing and effect on the wedding are crucial to the day flowing correctly. The problem is that when we try to add the church into today's normal timeline, it creates a bad experience for the guests. If you don't want to be in a church, then don't be in a church. Mom has to let that piece go. If you are in a church, it is critical to understand the proper flow of getting your guests from the church to the venue without leaving them in purgatory. In chapter five, I will tell you how to prepare your timeline to handle either scenarios

I love being married. It's so great to find that one special person you want to annoy for the rest of your life.

—Rita Rudner

8. *Receiving Line*

Don't do it. All you need is one uncle to talk to you for 5 minutes while everyone else stands there in line. Mix in time to talk to everyone later in the evening.

9. *Throwing the Bouquet / Throwing the Guarder*

Does anyone still do that?

10. *Wedding Cake*

You need to have a cake; don't be that bride that doesn't have it. The cake cutting is the starting gun for the party portion of the evening. BUT nobody really eats it. Everyone now wants individual desserts.

11. *Going Table to Table with Cookies*

This is a fun tradition. It does kill a significant amount of time for the newlyweds and forces the guests to stay in their seats. One out of every fifty weddings still does this.

12. *Dollar Dance*

Most brides don't even know what this is.

13. *Mom's Role*

Hey MOM, you have to understand that there are parts and pieces that just really don't happen very much anymore. And if your daughter doesn't want to do it, that's okay! They want to plan their own wedding, so, mom, you have to be willing to take a step back. The industry has changed and letting your daughter do it her way is okay. Allow her to have the wedding that SHE wants! But ladies, remember, when your mom got married 50 years ago, their moms did more of the planning than they did. That's how it was. Mom took control,

Grow old with me! The best is yet to be.

—Robert Browning

and mom and dad planned your wedding for you. So cut them a little slack.

Certainly, winning over mom is a big part of the wedding process. Having an experienced person in charge creates some faith and comfort. There has to be that connection between not only the bride, the groom, and the venue staff but also mom.

Often, moms jump onboard late and then show up for the final meetings. Everything you've decided over the course of a year, mom now wants to change and she's ready to fight for it. So this needs to be understood from the beginning. The bride needs to take the lead and let mom know where her place is in the process. Mom needs to be respected but also needs to be controlled.

*Love is our true destiny.
We do not find meaning of
life by ourselves alone—we
find it with another.*

—Thomas Merton

2.

THE 100% CLUB

What's the 100% Club, you ask? Well, I deal with five hundred couples annually and when brides and grooms come through the door, all of them tell me the same wrong stuff.

One hundred percent of the time they tell me, "I just got engaged," as if that's supposed to let me know they are not in any hurry. I understand that you just got engaged, but you don't have a lot of time to find a venue. The majority of couples have secured a venue within 25 days of their engagement.

One hundred percent of the time, I hear, "My list is big because I have to invite everybody." You don't have to invite everybody. You don't have to do anything. It's your wedding. Go for quality, not quantity; it's your decision.

One hundred percent of the time, they tell me that all of their guests are going to show up. Yup, magically you are the one bride that's going to invite 200 people and 200 people are going to show up.

*If I get married, I want
to be very married.*

—Audrey Hepburn

Wrong again. If you have a list of 50, maybe that could happen. Let's talk about those numbers. The higher you go in number, the bigger the drop-off rate.

For

100 invites, your loss percentage is 8%.

150 invites, your loss percentage is 13%.

200 invites, your loss percentage is 18%.

250 invites, your loss percentage is 21%.

Now, that is an annual average. Your loss rate is higher in the warmer months and lower in the colder months. More people say "yes" in March than in August.

One hundred percent of the time, I am told more people will show up on a Saturday than a Friday.

Swing and a miss. Let me share the data we have accumulated from premier wedding venues since 2014. More people RSVP "Yes" on Fridays than on Saturdays. That number grows by about 3% at 150 invites and up.

You may ask why, but I HAVE NO IDEA.

My guesses are

1. That they get to leave work early or miss work…completely.
2. Easier to go from work then sit around all day.
3. You don't screw up their weekend.

Oh, and guess what else. Go on, guess. Give up? More people RSVP "Yes" for Saturdays than for Fridays and then don't show up.

*I love you without knowing
how, or when, or from
where. I love you simply,
without problems or pride:
I love you in this way
because I do not know any
other way of loving but
this, in which there is no
I or you, so intimate that
your hand upon my chest
is my hand, so intimate
then when I fall asleep
your eyes close*

—Pablo Neruda, 100 Love Sonnets

One hundred percent of the time, I hear that your guests are going to drink me out of liquor. I am told that they are going to drink the entire time. They're all going to be drunk. "You've never seen my family drink!" Not true. They don't drink the way that you think they will, so one hundred percent of the time that actually doesn't happen.

One hundred percent of the time, their guests are going to eat all of the food. "We're going to run out of food; you've never seen my family eat!" If you're dealing with a venue that knows what they're doing, that is absolutely not the case.

One hundred percent of the time, it's going to rain. It is always going to rain. I always hear, "Well, with MY luck." Every single bride says, "It's going to rain on that day." Well, I can give you some actual statistics. In 11 years and roughly 2,200 ceremonies, not receptions, just ceremonies, I've moved 28 weddings inside. That's how infrequent it happens if you do it right. Now does that mean you're going to have the whole wedding outside? No. But you can actually have the 15-minute ceremony outside. The ceremony might start a little early or late, but it will happen.

Being deeply loved by someone gives you strength, while loving someone deeply gives you courage.

—Lao Tzu

3.

CHOOSING THE VENUE

Choosing the venue is obviously the most important thing you have to do. That's the first piece in this process. Once the venue is set, then you have a date, and you can act accordingly and progress accordingly with all of your other vendors. I tell people all the time to be very careful of a venue that has plenty of dates. Unless you are two years out, the better venues won't have plenty of dates. Usually, venues with a lot of dates available within two years are getting close to going under. Lately, we've had a real epidemic of venues going out of business, so you have to be very careful.

You need to find the right venue for you, no matter what that is. It has to feel right to you. Find the right theme. Find the right look. It's all very visual today. If it's not perfect for you, don't book it. Find the venue that is absolutely perfect.

One tip in picking the perfect venue is to make sure it is the right size.

*This is going to be a
great first wedding.*

—Wedding M.D.

Let's use one of my venues as an example. Let's pick the Cannery. Say a couple walks into the Cannery and they have 100 guests, but the Cannery seats 300 people. This creates a feeling similar to having the prom in a gymnasium.

It's not how a place looks on the day of, it's how the place feels. Of course, when you initially walk into a beautiful venue, you will be impressed. That feeling will last for the first hour maximum. After that, it's how the place feels and an empty venue feels just that—empty. So, yes, initially guests will say, "Wow, this place is great," but they will leave saying, "That wedding was okay." That's the last thing that anybody wants. Don't cram your guests into a venue that's too small, but don't put too few people in a venue that's too big. That's very very important. In talking to the venue, it's important to understand how they handle the small things. Do they have a person in place that's going to be in charge of your wedding from the beginning of the wedding to the end of the wedding? Talk with other brides that have been married there. Or go through the reviews to find out how they handle the small details. If they screw up dinner, everybody's going to know about it. But it's important to find out how they manage the emergencies and what systems they have in place to handle them.

What happens if the staff doesn't show up on that day? Or what happens if there are extreme weather conditions? What if it's raining; do they have umbrellas? That's simple. Do they have umbrellas to go out to the parking lot and get your guests? Those types of things are what you're going to want to make sure that a venue has contingencies for, not just the food. It's the little things that are going to make the venue stand out.

The greatest marriages are built on teamwork. A mutual respect, a healthy dose of admiration, and a never-ending portion of love and grace.

—Fawn Weaver

Listen, things may happen even if the venue is good, but if the venue is great you will never know there was an issue. Questioning the venue about their contract, I feel, is very important. Once you're locked into a contract with a venue, some of the venues will still go through price changes. You want to make sure that when you're locked in, the price cannot change. For example, some of the venues will change their menus. Again, you want to make sure that your menu is set and that any changes have to be approved through you. Understand all the things that are included in that contract! Very often, I have couples that will contact me and ask if things are included, just to check and see against another venue. It is never fun when they are closing in on their wedding and all of a sudden another chair adds a fee, a napkin is more money, or an hors d'oeuvre is extra. Don't assume what is included when you're picking a venue. Ask! Oftentimes, you will not be happy about what you find out.

Here are some dollar savers to keep in mind:

$ I am most often asked about tips on saving money with venues. Walking in and giving a venue a budget is a good idea. Some of the venues will put their pricing right online. I think that if they do, then they obviously have nothing to hide. Oftentimes, the venue will work hard to meet your budget, depending on the date.

$ Here's another money-saving idea. Don't walk into a venue with a particular date. You can ask them. I would be shocked if you let a venue pick your date, and they wouldn't be able to meet a certain budget. The venue might suggest a date in the winter or a holiday weekend where they know they're going to be slower.

$ The last dollar-saving tip in booking a venue is to see what's available within the same year. If you walk into a venue and you want to book a wedding that's only, say, four or five months out, you should be able to get

To find someone who will love you for no reason, and to shower that person with reasons, that is the ultimate happiness.

—Robert Brault (author)

a significant discount, as the odds of them filling that date with somebody else is minimal. This is the biggest money saver.

$ Two great dollar-saving bar tips

1. If your venue charges less for beer and wine, liquor's actually cheaper, especially well liquor. I would insist that they do a full bar for that same price. I'm sure that they will give in on that. A glass of wine and a bottle of beer is more expensive than a shot of vodka.

So it's actually less profitable for them to just serve beer and wine. I would insist on that all happening at the same price.

2. If you have a choice between a standard bar (beer, wine, well liquor) and a premium bar (top shelf), just remember one thing. People drink the most expensive free thing that you are pouring. Save your money; go standard!

Don't let a venue talk you into Sunday weddings. Sunday weddings suck. They are no fun whatsoever. Nobody wants to drink at a Sunday wedding. Unless it's a holiday weekend, avoid Sunday weddings at all cost. Don't avoid Friday weddings. Some venues will give you discount on Friday weddings. As I talked about earlier, more guests will show up at a Friday wedding than a Saturday wedding. Be very careful of wedding venues that do everything a la carte. Everything is an extra fee. When you do have a wedding venue that does everything a la carte, don't assume that **anything** will be included down the line. They're a la carte for a reason.

They're trying to get those little sales at the end, so make sure you have a very set contract when you get started. Don't be afraid to make your guest list smaller. That's the biggest driver of the wedding on

*Love is a promise; love
is a souvenir, once given
never forgotten; never
let it disappear.*

—John Lennon (musician)

most venues. Obviously, food is going to be the primary cost, and the more the people, the more expensive the wedding. You really want to take that into consideration and determine, "Do I want to have a good wedding with 200 people or a phenomenal wedding with 100 people?" Remember the 100% rule! Invite who you want. The last piece I'm going to talk about regarding booking weddings is the best time to book. Don't call a venue a year out looking for fall; everybody wants fall. So if you want an August through early November wedding, you're probably looking at two years out, so don't be surprised. Don't just settle on a venue because they have your date in the fall. As I said earlier, if you call a venue in February and they have the last weekend of September, which is one of the most popular weekends, there's probably a reason. Go and check out the venue; make sure that it's where you want to be. Summer weddings starting in early May are outstanding. Probably the toughest wedding temperature-wise is August, so keep that in mind. Winter weddings are absolutely beautiful; the photos that you get from winter weddings are incredible and many venues will do price discounts over the winter. There, you have it. Now, go get them.

*You know you're in love
when you can't fall asleep
because reality is finally
better than your dreams.*

—Dr. Seuss

4.

WHAT'S REALLY IMPORTANT

When Choosing Everyone Else

When choosing vendors, it's important not to overlook the obvious. In saying that, my goal is not to tell you whom to choose but things to keep in mind when you are making those decisions.

Picking Your DJ

Number one, you need to make sure that your DJ is at your venue and set up two hours in advanced. So if your ceremony is at three o'clock, the DJ needs to be there and set up at one. If your reception starts at five o'clock, then the DJ needs to be there and set up at three. You don't want to find out 15 minutes before the wedding starts that a speaker or microphone doesn't work. You want them to have time to fix it.

At my venues, this rule is mandatory. Two hours ahead of time. That's definitely something that you want to make sure that they put in their contract.

*The best and most
beautiful things in this
world cannot be seen or
even heard, but must be
felt with the heart.*

—Helen Keller

Don't listen to a DJ tell you, "Oh, I've never had a problem." That's a lie. Don't listen to a DJ tell you, "I never do that," or "It'll be fine." If it isn't fine, there is no time to fix it. You're talking about a huge impact on your wedding. I had a wedding in October of 2017 in which the DJ showed up 15 minutes after the ceremony was supposed to start. He showed up in gym shorts; it was awful. The wedding spiraled out of control because of it. I am positive that the bride is still pissed. Don't let the DJ drink. Make it as clear as you possibly can. They CANNOT DRINK at the reception. In fact, I would insist on putting it in the contract that the DJ will not consume any alcohol. Drunk DJs affect weddings in a very negative way. I would do the exact same thing with swearing, believe it or not. I insist that the DJs do not swear. I know some of the guests won't mind, but a lot of the guests, especially the older guests, get offended. You have to keep everybody happy. How are they dressed? That's something that when you meet with a new DJ you never ask. How do you usually dress on the day of the wedding? Are they in jeans and a t-shirt, which I've seen? Are they in tuxedos, or is it somewhere in between? How much advertising do they put up on their DJ booth? Sometimes, the DJ booths look like more like trade show booths than they do DJ booths. Who wants that visual in the middle of their wedding? I get it; they are trying to book more gigs, but that doesn't mean your wedding has to become a commercial for their product.

This is not KISS on tour, right? It is not a huge display where it's all about the DJ. You want a DJ to come in, control the room, play the music, and also play it at the right volume. Cranking the music as loud as you can does not make the room happy. You get a lot of people that will just leave. You don't want to give your guests a reason

Two souls with but a
single thought, Two
hearts that beat as one.

—John Keats

to leave the wedding early; this is already the fastest day of your life. You don't need to make it faster by driving everybody out with music cranking so loud that they can't hear. VERY IMPORTANT!!! If the music is wrong, that's your fault. Now that's funny because everybody says, "Well, I have to find the right DJ for the type of music."

They're all streaming music now. They all have all the music. Twenty-five years ago, you'd have to go pick the DJ based on the type of music he played. You'd have to find the right DJ and what his record collection looked like. That's not how it is now. They have all the music. So if you want to choose every song in the order in which you want those songs played, **then do that.** If you want to simply say, "Play dance music," and he doesn't play dance music that you like, that's your fault.

Picking Your Photographer

Let's assume in this section that you like your photographer's style/work. That has nothing to do with the factors I am going to give you.

Photographers can ruin weddings! Whenever I say that, everybody always says, "How can a photographer ruin a wedding?" The photographer is going to boss you around for the first two and a half hours of your day. They need to get certain shots. You ultimately want those shots, but you need to make sure, more than anything, that their personality will fit with not only your personality, but with those of the people that he or she will be working with that day. Their personality has a great deal to do with this and you need to think, "Am I really going to be comfortable?" They're part of your intimate group for your entire day.

You make me happier than I ever thought I could be, and if you let me, I will spend the rest of my life trying to make you feel the same way.

—Friends

Next, how quickly do they turn their pictures around? That's a biggie! No bride cares about when they're going to get their pictures, until the second the wedding ends. That's when she cares. "Oh, no, I don't care; take your time." And next thing you know, you're in the parking lot calling the photographer, "Do you have my pictures yet?" So you need to check into this. What is their average turnaround time? I would have in the contract that they guarantee that you're going to have your pictures by X date. That's certainly something that is reasonable and that I would highly recommend. Have they ever been to the venue before?

Huge question. If they have not been to the venue, are they going to go scout the venue? If a photographer walks in for the first time with you, your pictures are going to take a longgggggggg time.

Again, fastest day of your life. So the more time you spend away from the wedding with the photographer, the faster this day goes. Have very specific timelines with the photographer so they have a clear understanding of how long your pictures are going to take.

What pictures do you definitely want? Go and scout the venue together. Make sure that all those things are out on the table before you book the photographer.

Just like with the DJ, it's not just music.

With the photographer, it's not just pictures.

Choosing Your Videographers (Do I Need One?)

I don't see tons of videographers. It is something that went away years ago. Back in the 80s and 90s, everybody had a videographer.

*The highest happiness
on earth is the happiness
of marriage.*

—William Lyon Phelps

A lot of people think back to their own weddings and these huge cameras that everybody walked around. They filmed every single second of that wedding. And then you received a video to take home that lasted three hours and that you never watched. That's not what happens today.

What's popular now is trailers; it's a much shorter video. They last anywhere from 5 to 10 minutes in length. I really do think that they are nice to capture the wedding.

I watched my wedding video from 25 years ago. My daughter found it while moving and the people that were in the video are no longer around. Watching those type of moments brought back amazing memories. My personal advice is to capture those moments by hiring a professional.

So it serves a whole different purpose than just capturing the day, it captures the people in the moment. My personal experience made my opinion on a videographer change.

But just as with a photographer, consider their personality; it's very invasive. Ask them how they handle the day. Take a look at the equipment they use. Some use large equipment, and others use small. How intrusive are they during the wedding to get their footage?

Choosing Your Florist

When I talk about florists, I think about two things.

The first thing I think about is centerpieces. I can't tell you how many brides tell me they're going to make their own centerpieces.

Okay, you are not Martha Stewart!!!

Marriage is a mosaic you build with your spouse. Millions of tiny moments that create your love story.

—Jennifer Smith (author)

That's what this whole little section should be called: "You are not Martha Stewart."

Homemade centerpieces look like...*now wait for it,* they look like homemade centerpieces. That's what!! It is not inexpensive to do homemade centerpieces. To do what looks right, it will be cheaper to go with a florist.

They own the vases; they own all the expensive parts and pieces. If you buy the flowers, they let you use all of that stuff. Be very careful when doing your own centerpieces. You don't want to cheapen the wedding by having the focal point of the room be things that you bought at the Dollar General. Don't laugh; that's where some people go. The florists know what they are doing and do a great job. The second thing I think of is that bigger florists are full stagers.

So what I mean by this is there's so much visual in a wedding right now. The draperies, the bunting that hangs, bringing in furniture/antiques, and doing things around the room from the floor to the ceilings. That is now all part of what the florist does. They can make or break a room. That's a place where I wouldn't skimp on a budget. I think that going in with a budget is a great idea. Shopping the florist and really taking a dive into their visuals.

There are two people that I would make sure that you have given exact pictures and exact ideas. (Pinterest is a great place to find all those visuals.) One is the florist and the other one is your cake person. I wouldn't take any chances. Make sure that the florist is doing the delivery and the pickup. Make sure if they are doing all of the decorating that they're doing the setup and the take-down. That's not something you're going to want to do on wedding day. Find out what

*For the two of us, home
isn't a place. It is a person.
And we are finally home.*

—Stephanie Perkins

that process is and make sure you understand the costs. Some of the florists include it and others charge.

Choosing Your Desserts

A lot of people are telling me, "I'm not even going to have a wedding cake." Here's the problem with that. The cake cutting is really your starting gun for the reception; that's when people know to start to drink and dance and have fun. When you cut the cake, the dance music starts. Many of the older people will stay right at their table until you cut the cake. The problem is, when we don't cut cake, they will still stay there and wait at the table. In fact, I'll walk up to tables and say, "Ma'am, there is no cake." And she will say, "It's okay, I'll wait for the cake." And they'll just sit there. You definitely need a cake, but people love the individual desserts. I would definitely do a combination, even if it's a smaller wedding cake, just something to cut, something to start the party. It is the designated time for you to switch from the formalities of the wedding to just having a good time. That's what the cake cutting symbolizes more so than just a piece of cake. So try both. You can get individual desserts and cake.

A great tip for the cake is bring it back to the hotel. If you have people going back to the hotel at the end of the night, you have cake. I am sure that it's going to be the most delicious cake you've ever had in your entire life. I don't even think you'll need silverware. But it's fun. This way people will then eat the cake, but during the evening they will have individual desserts.

What Do I Do for Favors?

Why? Why do a favor? You're not doing anybody any favors with your favors. Unless you spend significant money, nobody cares what

*A wedding is an event,
but marriage is a life.*

—Myles Munroe

you're giving them. Add to your dessert table and put to-go boxes or bags out and let them take that home as the favor. But wasting money on a Koozie, a keychain, or some little individual glass makes no sense. It just goes on the shelf with their prom glasses, I guess. Oh, you don't have your prom glass anymore? Exactly! Forget the favors. You'll be doing them a favor.

Bridesmaids and Groomsmen

Okay, bridesmaids' dresses; just get it together please. Every bride reading this book right now, get it together. Don't kill your bridesmaids with some ridiculously colored, weird-cut dress that they obviously can never wear again. Keep it classic; keep it a color they can wear. Nobody can ever wear your fuchsia dress ever again. Just be a friend; these are your best friends, okay? Groomsmen, don't make them rent tuxes. Let them all go buy suits. You can walk into Jos. A. Bank, and when they have a suit special, buy one suit and get two for free. They'll sell you three of the same suit for the same money that you can rent a tuxedo for. Then, your groomsmen have a suit. Now, you buy them the socks and the tie and there's your groom's gift. Look at that; it's like magic. They have a suit that they can keep; they have socks and a tie. It's an easy groom's gift, and we're having fun.

We come to love not by finding a perfect person, but by learning to see an imperfect person perfectly.

—Sam Keen

5.

YOU ARE READY TO GET STARTED

So as we talked at the beginning about how timelines have changed from years ago and how the new timelines don't blend with the old, the most important thing outside of actually going through with it is making sure you don't leave your guests in an impossible situation. You have invited all of the closest people in your life to share this day with you; be considerate. Let's talk about the options for the ceremony that create the best situation for your guests to function in.

Option 1: In the Church

If you decide to get married in the church, you have two different timelines that you should follow to create a great day for everyone invited.

In the first timeline, you use a more traditional flow to your day. In this timeline, you get married early in the day, sometime around noon. Your ceremony will end around 1:00–1:15 PM. In this case, you can opt to doing a receiving line.

When someone else's happiness is your happiness, that is love.

—Lana Del Ray

You then allow your guests plenty of time in between the ceremony and the reception by starting the reception around 5 PM. That gives your guests plenty of time in between so that it's very obvious that they do not leave the church and go directly to the reception hall. If you don't leave a significant amount of time, some guests, especially the older ones, will leave the church and go directly to the reception. If this happens, most of the time the hall won't even have people there to greet them yet. The venue might not even be open. You do not want to leave your guests in a four-hour limbo. But if you do, make it very deliberate so that they understand what to do and that they understand that they are not going to the venue. If I have a five-hour break in between, it's pretty obvious to me that I would just show up at the starting time. In fact, the older guests are used to this and oftentimes figure out where to gather. I would like to offer a warning. Your friends are going to find a bar and drink for the next 4–5 hours.

That's option one. Unfortunately, most people don't want to do that; it just sucks to be left in limbo.

In timeline two, you have to fix the wedding by limiting the time in between and extending the cocktail hour. Now I'm going to tell you that a one-hour cocktail hour is too short anyway. We're going to talk about that in a minute.

Let's walk you through another case.
1. 2:00 PM, ceremony in a church. Your ceremony will end 3:00–3:15 PM.
2. Guests leave the church by 3:30 PM.
3. Your guests arrive at the venue by 4:00 PM.

A successful marriage requires falling in love many times, always with the same person.

—Mignon McLaughlin

4. Your guests immediately go into cocktail hour. The key to this is a 4–6 PM cocktail hour that lasts TWO HOURS.

5. You start taking pictures at 3:30 PM and continue till 4:30 PM.

6. You leave the church and head to the reception hall at 4:45 PM.

7. You arrive at 5:00 PM and still have an hour of cocktail hour with your guests until 6:00 PM.

Note: This works perfectly. Keep in mind, you DO NOT do a receiving line at the church; you use your cocktail hour to greet your guests. This is tremendously better for your guests and it allows them to go directly from the church to the reception hall without being left in limbo.

Option 2: At the Venue Sight

This option is very similar to our second church timeline, but even better for your guests. In this timeline, let's say the ceremony happens at 4:00 PM. A ceremony at the venue is going to take roughly 15 minutes. When the ceremony ends, if you have a two-hour cocktail hour, you again now have the ability to do a one-hour photoshoot and then mingle with your guests for the remaining hour.

This again gives you the opportunity to walk around, meet and greet your guests, say hello to all the older folks, and do all the things that you would have during the receiving line. Thank them for coming, get them to say how happy they are for you, allow them their time with you. They're all looking to thank you and to tell you how wonderful you look and that they're so happy for you. Allow them the opportunity to do that.

Now why is this option a great choice? Number one, your guest's don't have to worry about anything. Number two, the venue is going

Being someone's first love may be great, but to be their last is beyond perfect.

—Unknown

to do a better job of controlling the guests' drinking. This also creates an amazing pre-party for the wedding, which is really what you're trying to accomplish. You're trying to take a day that's going to go superfast and stretch it. So an extended cocktail hour, in my opinion, is a must, regardless.

I always recommend an abundance of hors d'oeuvres during cocktail hour. You want lots of things being passed, not just a little table with cheese. Go big with it. Have anywhere from eight to ten different hors d'oeuvres. Now the number of hors d'oeuvres will depend on the venue, your caterer, and the price. You definitely want lots of food coming around. Another recommendation is that I love live music during cocktail hour. It's very inexpensive.

For $200–$300 dollars, you can have somebody, such as an acoustic artist or pianist, play for the two-hour cocktail hour. It will change the entire event. It adds so much life. It's charming and it's a huge visual.

Their presence creates a pre-party. That's what we're trying to do. We're trying to stretch this event. So now we've gone from church into the cocktail hour. We have two hours. We have plenty of drinks. We have plenty of hors d'oeuvres being passed. We have live music. All things that you'll thank me for after your wedding. Keep in mind, as far as the bar goes during this event, I know some venues will allow shots. More and more sites are getting away from it. I would encourage you NOT to allow shots. Drunk people at weddings act like drunk people, which is really a bad situation. This is a perfect time to talk about the real villains and the people who ruin weddings on a regular basis. And that would be the groomsmen. They are the worst. So I'm going to give you a couple of tips right now

Once in a while, right in the middle of an ordinary life, love gives us a fairytale.

—Unknown

with regard to groomsmen. Let me explain what the difference is between bridesmaids and groomsmen. When a bridesmaid wakes up on the morning of the wedding, she will look at the bride and be so excited because it's the bride's day. "We're all so happy for you. You are the bride, and it's your day. Whatever you want, we can do for you." When the groomsmen wake up, they're super excited because it's their day and they want to do shots on their day.

Here Is the Problem

1. If they're drunk for the ceremony, it's difficult to even get them down the aisle and it becomes a joke. It affects the wedding negatively.

2. Pictures are now impossible because they want to just screw around. They want to continue to get drunk. Pictures will take twice as long.

3. They start to lose their buzz during pictures, so during cocktail hour they get super drunk.

4. Usually, that means they don't eat dinner, because they don't want to lose their buzz again.

5. And now they're full-on drunken fools for the rest of the wedding. If you have drunk groomsmen, the next day the guests will not be talking about the bride. They will be talking about the groomsmen. And that's what'll happen.

So how do we fix this? And here's the greatest tip that I'm going to give. Every bride and groom need to listen.

If the groomsmen are drinkers, I want the groom to take the groomsmen out after the rehearsal dinner and get them shit-face hammered drunk, just hammered drunk. Make it a challenge to get them as

*When you realize you want
to spend the rest of your
life with somebody, you
want the rest of your life to
start as soon as possible.*

—When Harry Met Sally

drunk as possible. Why, you ask? We want them recovering from their hangover just in time for the ceremony. We don't want them waking up to drink all day. We want them eating and drinking coffee. So do yourself a favor and get your groomsmen hammered drunk the day before your wedding. That's the greatest advice I can give every bride and every groom.

Warning! Be careful! Sometimes, the bridesmaids get a little sneaky and they'll try to feed the bride too many mimosas and that type of thing. I've had some horror stories with drunk brides. That's just something that I would keep an eye out for, a little bit lesser of an eye. But be careful! Okay, so now we've been through cocktail hour, it's lasted for two hours. It's been wonderful. We've had live music. We've had drinks and we've made it through pictures. You got your groomsmen drunk the night before, so they're not too out of control on the day of the wedding. Now, it's time for everybody to get to their seats.

Let's talk about seating charts and how to seat people. Your guests, no question, have already gone around and tried to find their seats from the seating chart.

Number one, you have to do a seating chart. Do not be the person who thinks, "I'm just going to let my guests pick their own seats." NO NO NO. The movie theater effect takes over. What's that? Let me explain. Nobody likes to sit right next to someone at the movie theatre, so they leave one empty seat.

Let's apply this to your wedding. Say you have a table of eight and the first couple sits down. The second couple will sit down and inevitably leave one empty seat. Now, the table of eight, at best, just became

*Every great love starts
with a great story...*

—Nicholas Sparks

a table of six. You'll need tons of extra seating because you'll have empty spaces. You won't be able to control it. You don't want a venue rolling tables in during your wedding because you don't have enough seats. Which is exactly what will happen if you just let the guests pick their own seats.

Don't let a seating chart stress you out; it does not matter who sits with whom. Nobody's going to yell and scream at one another if you seat them together. It's a wedding; please don't overthink it. Nobody's going to scream from one table to another; it's never happened. People are going to sit, and they're going to eat, and then they're going to get up. The key is to make sure you have the right number of tables. What does that mean? Many venues will just take the easiest way out. You have 120 people. "I'm going to set up 15 tables of 8, and that's it. It's a wrap." Well, the room doesn't look right with 15 tables of 8. Maybe the room looks better with 20 tables in it, while 20 tables of 6 will still get you to 120 guests. Make your room look right and then reverse engineer your list. Meaning the room looks best with 20 tables, then seat your 120 guests, or 115 guests, or 137 guests, using 20 tables. Make the room look right, then design the list around the room, not the other way around. Get a seating chart that you can move. What's very popular now is the old window panes and things of that nature, not individual cards. Number one, they fall over. Number two, you don't want to put a seating chart in an entranceway because people are sheep and when they open the door, the guests will stop. You will create a line at the entrance or you will create this pile of people in a corner. You want to take a seating chart and put it in the center of a room, or on a dance floor. Somewhere that people can still come in, still move around, and then before introductions,

It doesn't matter if the guy is perfect or the girl is perfect, as long as they are perfect for each other.

—Sean (Good Will Hunting)

move it to its permanent home. You want to have something that you can move. A great touch is to have food on the tables when your guests take their seat. They're trapped at their table. That's the one time a guest is trapped. We've all been guests at weddings, and we've all sat at the tables during the speeches, toasts, introductions, dances, and we've all wished that the speeches, toasts, introductions, and dances were over, right? Nobody cares about any of that except for your immediate family. So you're a guest, you take a seat, introductions start. By the time you are actually eating, it could be 45 minutes later. Put some food on each table, something that guests can pick at. We do cutting boards with food sucks as fruit, vegetables, hummus, and tapenade. I don't care if it's a loaf of bread; pick something that they can pick and eat.

Do not close your bar during introductions and dinner. It's confusing; nobody gets it; it's a pain in the ass. If you want to save money, shut your bar an hour early, but don't do it in the middle of dinner. Plan a timeline, but you will have to be very careful. So we've done cocktail hour and we've had a great time. Everybody is seated. They're happy at their table because there's food on the table. You're doing introductions, you're into dances, and now you get to the speeches. That whole timeline really needs to be planned, and it's very important that you understand how long your bridesmaids and groomsmen are going to talk. I've had situations where groomsmen go on for 45 minutes. A bridesmaid follow that up with a 15-minute speech. Now we're at our table for an hour because the groomsman thought he was funny. Give them a time limit. Tell them 5 minutes. The popular things now are the dances or songs by the bridesmaids and groomsmen. And that's fine as long as they communicate it to you or the

To be your friend was all I ever wanted; to be your lover was all I ever dreamed.

—Valerie Lombardo

venue. I'll tell you, if you want hot food at your wedding, you'll have to control the bridesmaids and the groomsmen. Most venues will set your food at the beginning of the second speech. So if that speech goes for 45 minutes, you're in really big trouble. Control what that looks and feels like; give them a timeline. Especially if they're going to be drinking, give them a time limit.

Let's talk about dinner. "I want a plated dinner," said no guest at any wedding ever. Plated dinners take too long. You have two options with a plated dinner. You can take food that probably started out good, let's give every venue the benefit of the doubt, and you pre-plated it, put a lid on it, and stuck it in a warmer. It sits in that warmer until it can be handed out to everybody, so everybody gets moderately warm, probably overcooked food. Or you plate as you go, which is if the venue has enough space. They can plate as they go, but it takes forever. You're going to have your guests trapped at their tables. I get it, you like the visual. You watch the Hallmark wedding movie and they had a plated meal. Every person in the audience got their meal at the exact same time, which is really a phenomenal Hallmark movie. I'm sure I've seen it; it's the one with a prince and a princess. But that's a fairytale; you don't have a staff of 300 people serving 300 guests. What's going to happen is you're going to be done eating and the last table doesn't even have their food yet. I'll tell you what else happens. No matter what the guest gets, they want what the other person has. More than likely they've forgotten what they've even ordered, which happens 90% of the time. They end up swapping meals: "I'll take your chicken, you take my steak." It doesn't do anything for the event.

*When someone loves you,
the way they talk about
you is different. You feel
safe and comfortable.*

—Jess C. Scott?(The Intern)

If you have a buffet and the food is good, the guests can go for seconds and thirds. They can try what they want. More importantly, it's going to move quick. Make sure that whomever you're getting your food from, you request a full tasting. You don't want to do two dishes or three dishes. They're obviously going to give you things that they can't screw up. Try everything, it's important! Having a plated meal is not nearly as important as having a quality dinner that your guests truly enjoy. Lots of hors d'oeuvres is important; even fun surprises with food is great. Late-night food service of pizzas, or McDonald's, or anything that people would eat at the end of the night is more important than the fancy look of a plated dinner. Do your guests a favor and don't make them sit there. Then, just enjoy the rest of the wedding, cut your cake, and dance!

Love you not only for what you are, but for what I am when I am with you. I love you not only for what you have made of yourself, but for what you are making of me. I love you for the part of me that you bring out.

—Elizabeth Barrett Browning

6.

BRIDES BEWARE: HAZARDS AHEAD

Hazard 1

The stations wedding. Anybody that has been to a fundraiser, or watched a Hallmark movie, sees this wedding. The food is out everywhere and everybody is just having a good time. Or, quite frankly, if you've been to a nice fundraiser with food out with hors d'oeuvres all over the place, it really does seem like a fun event.

The problem with this is that it is almost impossible to control. I'll give you the visual. Imagine you're at a beautiful wedding and you go through the hors d'oeuvres. You sit everybody at their tables because you have to do your introductions, dances, and speeches. Then the venue puts out stations at each corner of the room. You have a carving station, a pasta station, a beautiful seafood station. Maybe you have a salad station wonderfully done. Then the food goes out and everything's finished. The speeches end and all your 140 guests get up, all at the same time, to go to these stations. Now, all you have are squiggly lines throughout the venue because the guests refuse not

*Everything is clearer
when you're in love.*

—John Lennon

to stand in line. They go to the first station and they get a little plate of food. They then sit at the table and soon go to the second station for a plate of food. They go back to the table and do this time and time again. And then they come back and eat cold food after they stood in line for 45 minutes. It doesn't work. If you're at a fundraiser, you never sit 150 people down all at the same time. You might have announcements and things that happen throughout the course of the evening. But you do not actually formally sit everybody down, every single guest, and then unleashing them on the food. If you want to do a stations wedding, just keep in mind, you can't do introductions, speeches, and toasts. You can't sit everybody at the same time. You can sprinkle that stuff in throughout the course of the evening, but you have to be very careful that a venue knows how to do that. Or else it's no fun for anybody.

Hazard 2

Kids ruin weddings. I'm sorry to be the one that tells you this, but kids do ruin weddings! I get it. "I have to invite my sister's kids." Kids ruin weddings. I'm not saying you shouldn't invite them; that's up to you. There's a lot of sugar, there's a lot of music for the kids, and there's a lot of drinking for the adults. Kids run around and they dominate the dance floor. By the time it's dance time, they're running around the dance floor so much that they essentially push the adults off the dance floor. I know, "not your family"; that's what everybody tells me. Guess what? It happens to every family. They run around the venue and their parents yell at them to stop running. Ultimately, whomever they're with will leave early and they don't get to really enjoy the wedding because they had to watch their kids the whole time. Or, even worse, the parents really enjoy the wedding, and that

*The goal of marriage
is not to think alike,
but to think together.*

—Renee Combs

means everybody else is watching their kids. Bring them to the ceremony, if you want. If you want them to stay for dinner. Figure out transportation, rent a hotel room, get a babysitter, do what you need to do. Get rid of the kids. Get rid of the children. Okay?

Hazard 3

As we talked about earlier, make sure your timeline is spot on. Control the speeches. Control the photographers and DJs. Those are things that can get out of control. I'm sure you'd like to have warm food. I'm sure that you would like to be in cocktail hour. Those things are going to be controlled primarily by two things: the speeches and how long the photos take with the photographer. Make sure that that's a big point that you're aware of.

Hazard 4

Don't feel obligated. Don't feel obligated to do a receiving line. Don't feel obligated to be in a church.

Don't feel obligated to take pictures for two hours, or throw a bouquet, or do a favor. Don't feel obligated to do any of that. Don't let mom force you into a rehearsal. Rehearsals are for churches, not for venues. You're rehearsing stepping left and right. Don't be forced into anything. These are all things that I want every bride to know.

Hazard 5

Drunk Groomsmen. The best piece of advice that this book has given is get the groomsmen drunk the day before the wedding. If you want a nice, peaceful wedding day, get the groomsmen hammered drunk the night before. You will thank me later.

Marriage is not just about love. It is more than that. It is about commitment, giving, taking, and understanding.

—Wedding M.D.

Hazard 6

What nobody wants to talk about is cancellations. I lose about 10 weddings a year and it's really because of a break up. Let's face it, terrible things happen to people leading up to weddings, to family members, to jobs. Things that nobody likes to talk about. Sicknesses and catastrophic events end up forcing you to cancel or have a strong effect on your weddings. Something you might want to think about is wedding insurance. I try to tell every couple about buying wedding insurance. It's like trip insurance. On a $20,000 wedding, you might be looking at $200–$300 and it reimburses you for everything that you've paid out of pocket for the wedding. It doesn't cover change of heart, it doesn't cover cheating, but that's really not why weddings get cancelled.

It's a pretty horrific thing, so as part of my beware, I'm going to throw wedding insurance in there. It's really something that people should look at. You can go online and Google "wedding insurance." There's lots of different companies out there, very reputable companies, that sell it. I think that it's certainly worth it.

Hazard 7

Don't miss your day worrying. The one thing I want to make sure happens is that when the day of your wedding comes, no matter how big of a control freak you've been during the process, no matter how much mom has gotten involved, no matter what things have happened through the whole process that have made you angry, or happy, or sad, just enjoy the day of the wedding! Let the venue take control. Whatever is going to happen at this point is going to happen. Have fun. Enjoy the process. It's the fastest day of your life. Make it

The most important four words for a successful marriage: I'll do the dishes.

—Carrie Sagroi

feel like the longest day. Don't sweat the small stuff; just go with the flow on the day of the wedding, and hopefully this little bit of advice has given you some guidance in what to pick, and what to choose, and what questions to ask.

What greater thing is there for two human souls, than to feel that they are joined for life, to strength each other in all labor, to rest on each other in all sorrow, to minister to each other in silent unspeakable memories at the moment of the last parting?

—George Eliot

Have a wonderful wedding.

*Success in marriage
does not come merely
through finding the
right mate, but through
being the right mate.*

—Barnett R. Brickner